The GiBBON'S in DECLiNE

but the HORSE is STABLE ...

The GiBBON'S in DECLiNE but the HORSE is STABLE ...

anthropoemorphic
ramblings from

MAUREEN LiPMAN

ROBSON
BOOKS

First published in the United Kingdom in 2006 by
Robson Books
151 Freston Road
London
W10 6TH

An imprint of Anova Books Company Ltd

Design: Neil Stevens, Abby Franklin, Lee-May Lim

ISBN 1 86105 969 8

A CIP catalogue record for this book is available from the British Library

10 9 8 7 6 5 4 3 2 1

Reproduction by Anorax Imaging
Printed and bound by *Partenaires Book*®, France

This book can be ordered direct from the publisher.
Contact the marketing department, but try your bookshop first

www.anovabooks.com

illustrators

Gerald Scarfe
Jan Pienkowski
Posy Simmonds
Gray Jolliffe
Mac (Stan McMurtry)
Phillip Hood
Bill Tidy
Maureen Lipman
Amy Rosenthal
Natalie Percy

Dedicated to the memory of

Jack Rosenthal
Willis Hall
Denis Quilley
Sandy Scott
Jonathan James Moore
Dan Crawford
Lynn Shindler
and Edith Butler

introduction

Why Animal poems? Why Cartoons? Why Myeloma? Why me? Are you sitting continently? Then I'll begin.

When my late husband, Jack Rosenthal, was diagnosed with Myeloma, neither he nor I knew how serious it was. To be honest we didn't really know *what* it was. We found out the hard way.

We found out through great trials and many errors, through experts who gave good bedside manner but no content and experts with the bedside manner of a wardrobe but brains the size of Walberswick. We got zapped by Radiotherapy and marooned on Planet Chemo, fought the most intense battle of our lives in Intensive Care at the Royal Marsden Hospital, celebrated glorious remission, then faced imminent death, within the space of three months.

It may not have changed a thing, I know, but I wish I'd got to know more about what Myeloma consultant Dr Gareth Morgan calls 'The Cinderella Disease'. He calls it that, not because it's ugly, though it is, not because it transforms itself, though it can, not because it lets you live happily ever after, because it doesn't, but because, of the three major blood cancers, Leukaemia, Lymphoma and Myeloma, it is the one which is least acknowledged, least discussed and has least money spent on it.

The anomaly is that early diagnosis is vital but difficult. The disease presents symptoms in confusingly different ways. Jack had violent back pain ... *'Arthritis?'*. Some others I've met started with exhaustion, *'take more exercise'*, eye problems, *'change your specs and eat carrots'*, rashes, *'lay off wheat ... try this skin cream'* and even, in the case of one sufferer, Ivy, who has lived with Myeloma for sixteen years, wobbly knees, *'give up the Guinness!'*.

All the royalties from the sale of this book will go to the International Myeloma Foundation UK because it's a small organisation with a vast heart and the cleanest arteries of any charity I've known. Any money raised for IMF is ploughed straight back into patient seminars, research and their 24-hour Helpline.

The Gibbon's in Decline but the Horse Is Stable came about as a by-product of Jack's two-year-long battle with Myeloma. As you can imagine, I wasn't sleeping too well during this period and on the long journeys to visit him in hospital in Sutton and Wimbledon, a fifty-mile round trip, my mind was racing like Schumacher on amphetamines. Instinctively, as a panic diversion one day, I started making up what I called Daft Verses. The first was:

> *The Lemur cub was crying.*
> *'Why so sad?' I asked her*
> *'I'm a homesick Lemur, with a broken femur,*
> *And me mum's in Madagascar.'*

It took me all the way from Muswell Hill to Hammersmith to create that complex masterpiece of content and style and it struck me that for the whole forty-five minutes, I had thought of little else. I was on to something. While I was with Jack, I was totally in the present and dealing with whatever was needed. All my energy had to be saved for him. On the way home, instead of going through the hell of *Would it have been better if?* and *Should I have changed doctors mid-stream?* I tackled first, the fetishistic Zebra, second, the oscillating ocelet, and later, I put myself into a decent state of REM sleep by wrestling with a gay fruit-bat. Intellectual it wasn't, all-consuming it most definitely was.

Over the course of two years both lean and fat, I chalked up nearly fifty verses. I guess they fall somewhere between McGonnegal and Milligan, and *Poetry in Andrew Motion* they're never going to be, but to me, they do represent the mask of comedy propping up the mask of tragedy. Sweet and sour, Yin and Yang. Restoring proportion to a life corkscrewed by fate. I believe it was Alan Ayckbourn who said, 'Comedy is tragedy with interruptions.' No one knew it more than Jack. His entire output of plays, all 150 of them, juxtaposed the pain of laughter and the laughter behind the pain. He's left us with such sweet sorrow.

After his death, in 2003, I never wrote, or indeed thought of, another Daft Verse. It was only this year that I looked them over with a view to putting them together with cartoons in the hope of raising some money for the IMF. I only called cartoonists whom I knew and revered personally to a man, to a *human*, even: Gerald Scarfe, Jan Pienkowski, Gray Jolliffe, Mac (Stan McMurtry), Philip Hood, Bill Tidy and Posy Simmonds. My daughter, Amy Rosenthal, and our friend Natalie Percy also contributed beautiful illustrations. They all said yes immediately and pushed aside their packed schedules to produce, gratis, the delightful, anthropomorphic illustrations you see before you. 'If you want something doing,' my dear old dad used to say, 'ask a busy person.' Thank you to all of them. I'm very grateful.

I had thought of calling the book *I'm Not Averse...* but when I saw Gerald's free-falling Gibbon, the whole title came to me in a flash – but then, I am of a certain age. For those of you who have bought this book, I thank you, too. I hope you enjoy it and that it makes you laugh and groan ... and for those of you who are thumbing through it in the Jewish Humour section of the bookshop, which is, undoubtedly where they'll stick it, you are penny-pinching and a fool to yourself and if you don't buy it you will get fungal warts and excess belly button fluff.

Meanwhile, I now have my own diversionary animal in the shape of Diva, the four-month-old, Basenji puppy. She's the bark-less dog of the Congo. I got her from Ealing. She's a bitch, but I love her. It's hard to be pessimistic with a puppy in the house ... Hell, I think I feel a bit of Doggerel coming on ...

Maureen Lipman, 2006

'i want to sing Otello,'
Said a classical Flamingo.
'Haven't you heard,
   you're a fat, pink bird,
'Not Placido Domingo?'

An adolescent Leopard
For a panther had 'the hots'
With acne pill and Clearasil
He tried to change his spots.

Illustration: Posy Simmonds

Benobos, apes, gorillas
(Their collective name is Simian)
Meet bookish gangs of
    orang-utans
To read Keats' poem 'Endymion'.

Illustration: Mac

Two business-minded jumbo Prawn
A lady and her daughter,
Set up stalls 'neath three brass ball
— A prawn shop, under water!

Illustration: Gray Jolliffe

Never cross a Rhino,
if criticised, he's nasty.
With scent of musk, he'll use
  his tusk
To give you rhino-plasty.

Illustration: Phillip Hood

The creatures enter two by two,
Old Noah stops and thinks
Makes a beeline for a single feline
Saying, 'Ah! The missing Lynx.'

Illustration: Jan Pienkowski

A Buffalo i'm proud to know,
An enterprising fella,
Sometimes barters plum tomatoes
For Buffalo Mozzarella.

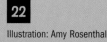

Illustration: Amy Rosenthal

Rhett Beaver told his lady wife
'Our logs are in a jam.
You keep the flat, the kids and
the cat,
But frankly, i won't give the Dam.

Illustration: Gray Jolliffe

Raymond was a Hippo,
His birthday was in May,
When every mate would ullulate
'Hippo Hippo, Ray!'

Illustration: Bill Tidy

A fetishistic Zebra
Declared, with mane a-tossing,
'i like to pose in women's clothes,
'Cos i'm a Zebra crossing!'

Illustration: Posy Simmonds

Lemmings fear to travel,
For weeks they mull it over.
'We don't mind Finland,
  or anywhere inland,
But we hate the Cliffs of Dover!'

30
Illustration: Gerald Scarfe

'Those nosey Brontë sisters'
The Pterodactyls chorus.
'Upon yon moors, they
    peer through doors -
i'm sure that Brontësaurus!'

Illustration: Mac

A team of Dolphin builders
Were feeling pangs of guilt,
with work protracted
   they sub-contracted
And the place got Porpoise-built

Illustration: Gray Jolliffe

Said the Chipmunk, 'i'm a villain.
World art fraud is my scheme.
i foiled the police, with a
    masterpiece,
i call Chip Munch's *The Scream*

Illustration: Phillip Hood

Voles are workaholics,
Stoats tend to be skivers.
A tall Giraffe does 'owt for a laugh
And Ferrets fart for fivers.

Illustration: Jan Pienkowski

My Parrot loved Miss Hepburn,
Saw all her films twice-nightly.
Found her epiphanies in *Breakfast
at Tiffany's*
And called herself 'Polly Golightly'.

40

The Panda was provocative
And almost risked pneumonia,
Broke all the rules, peed in the pool
And caused near pand-ammonia.

Illustration: Gerald Scarfe

A Border pup and a Burmese cat
Once ruled a tribe of Frogs.
'Beyond a joke', their subjects croak
'it's reigning cats and dogs!'

Illustration: Gray Jolliffe

The Lemur cub was lonesome,
'Why so sad?' i ask her.
'i'm a homesick Lemur
   with a broken femur
And my mum's in Madagascar.'

Illustration: Amy Rosenthal

A Porcupine from Swansea
Loved a pig from Tunnoch Brae,
They sang the blues in separate
 zoos
And pork-u-pined away.

Illustration: Posy Simmonds

n woke up
morning...

My Ocelot would laugh a lot
And when he was elated
His fur would shake, his nostrils
  quake
Until he oscillated.

Illustration: Gray Jolliffe

i'm a little Unicorn
More mythical than macho
For i was born, with a unique horn
So momma calls me Satchmo

Illustration: Maureen Lipman

The Tortoise streaked into the lead
The Hare was under stress.
i made my bid and lost ten quid,
A bad Hare day, i guess.

Illustration: Gerald Scarfe

'That Horse in front,' the Whisperer
  breathed,
'Why don't you just sneak up on it.'
The stallion shied and then replied
'i say, can you speak up a bit?'

Illustration: Gray Jolliffe

A Swan, whose babes had flown
   the nest,
Wept beneath her wing;
'For goodness sake, what does
   it take
To make a cygnet ring?'

Illustration: Natalie Percy

A nervous Wolf was training
With the army in the Gulf.
On Red Alert his eyes would spurt
A case of Crying Wolf?

Illustration: Gerald Scarfe

A giant Caterpillar's son,
Horned as a Visigoth,
Caterwauled 'i am appalled,
To think i'll be a Moth.'

Illustration: Gray Jolliffe

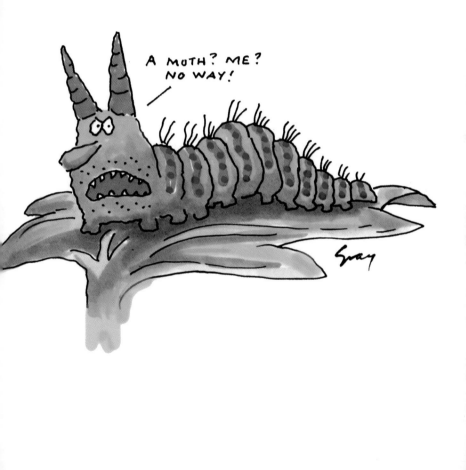

'Take that!' said the Dodo.
The scientist just blinked.
'Here in Mauritius
  it isn't propitious
To call a girl extinct.'

Illustration: Gerald Scarfe

Said dentist Phil MCavity,
'Open wide please, Keith
You've spat and rinsed and
 i'm convinced
You're lion, through your teeth.'

Illustration: Posy Simmonds

A Sloth was hanging from a tree,
imbibing large Sloe gins,
'i'm hellish proud,' he said out loud,
'To be one of the deadly sins.'

Illustration: Gray Jolliffe

There was a dandy Prairie Wolf
in panama and goatee,
Who'd roam the hills and tilt
  at mills
So they called him Don Coyote.

Illustration: Posy Simmonds

The Elephant had a make-over
The stylist made her punk.
A pachyderm with a crappy perm
Singing 'i was Born in a Trunk'.

Illustration: Phillip Hood